POINT OF IMPACT

Revised and Updated

Heinemann Library
Chicago, Illinois

The Printing Press

A Breakthrough in Communication

© 2000, 2006 Heinemann Library
a division of Reed Elsevier Inc.
Chicago, Illinois

Customer Service 888-454-2279
Visit our website at www.heinemannraintree.com

Designed by Tokay Interactive Ltd. (www.tokay.co.uk)
Printed in China by WKT Ltd

10 09 08 07 06
10 9 8 7 6 5 4 3 2 1

New edition ISBNs:1-40349-143-7 (hardcover)
                  1-40349-152-6 (paperback)

The Library of Congress has cataloged the first edition as follows:
Tames, Richard.
      Printing press : a breakthrough in communication / Richard Tames.
            p.cm. — (Point of impact)
      Includes bibliographical references and index.
      Summary: Surveys the development of the printing press, from advances in Asia and Gutenberg's work in Germany to the profound impact of printing on civilizatoin in general.
      ISBN 1-57572-418-9 (library binding)
      1. Printing—History—Juvenile literature. [1. Printing—History.]. I. Title. II. Series.

Z124 .T36 2000
686.2—dc21
                                                    00-026084

Acknowledgments
The publishers would like to thank the following for permission to reproduce photographs: Bridgeman: p. **9**,(British Library) p. **6**, (Christie's) p. **5**, (The Stapleton Collection) p. **11**, (Trinity College) p. **8**; Corbis: p. **29** (Chuck Savage), pp. **18**, **21**, **28**, (Michael Maslan) p. **14**, (Underwood & Underwood) p. **4**; Corbis/Bettman: p. **28**; Mary Evans Picture Library: pp. **7**, **12**; National Maritime Museum: p. **15**; Tames, Richard: pp. **19**, **22**, **23**, **26**; The British Library: pp. **10**, **20**; University of Reading Library: pp. **16**, **17**; Victoria and Albert Museum: p. **13.**

Cover photograph reproduced with permission of Bridgeman Art Library.

The publishers would like to thank Stewart Ross for his help in the preparation of this book.

Contents

Some words are shown in bold, **like this**. You can find out what they mean by looking in the Glossary.

Made in Mainz

Man with a mission

Johannes Gutenberg (about 1398–1468) spent his life on a great project. Before his time, books were copied slowly, by hand. This made them incredibly expensive. Gutenberg's idea was to combine two well-known processes. The first was printing things, such as playing cards, using carved wooden blocks; the second was crushing grapes in a press to release their juice. He combined these two techniques, added further inventions, and created the brand-new technology of printing. His plan was to produce entire books printed from separate pieces of metal **type**. Unlike wooden blocks, these could be broken down after printing and used again. Sadly, Gutenberg's dream was fulfilled not by himself but by his business partner.

Technical problems

Gutenberg was born in Mainz, Germany, and trained as a goldsmith. A highly skilled metalworker, he invented an adjustable mold so that he could **cast** uniform pieces of metal type—representing different letters of the alphabet—quickly and in large numbers. He perfected an **alloy** of tin, lead, and **antimony**, which melted easily, flowed evenly, and cooled quickly. To hold separate letters as lines of print that stayed straight under pressure, he designed an adjustable frame. Finally, he improved traditional presses to apply pressure evenly across paper, and he developed a new type of oil-based ink.

A replica of Gutenberg's printing press is on display in his original workshop in Mainz, Germany.

Business problems

Around 1450 Gutenberg went into partnership with a lawyer, John Fust, who loaned him money for a printing business. In 1453 he began working on a three-volume Bible. This progressed very slowly, and the partnership with Fust broke down in 1455. Gutenberg could not pay back the money to Fust, so he had to surrender the press. Fust and his son-in-law Peter Schoffer, Gutenberg's assistant, actually finished the first printed Bible, but it is still known as Gutenberg's Bible.

Print against pen

One single, hand-copied Bible would take a **scribe** about four years to finish. Twenty men produced 450 Gutenberg Bibles in one year. Therefore, each Bible was produced 90 times faster and cost only one-tenth as much as a hand-copied version. Printing meant books were no longer only for the rich. Most **literate** people could now gain access to books. Instead of relying on a priest or scribe to tell them what was in a book, people could read for themselves. New ideas and new information meant new challenges to old ideas and the people who held them.

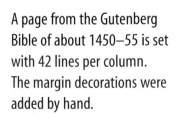

A page from the Gutenberg Bible of about 1450–55 is set with 42 lines per column. The margin decorations were added by hand.

Asian Advances

Sacred signs

Printing from carved wooden blocks, to reproduce religious writings and images, was being used in China, Korea, and Japan by the 8th century C.E. Rulers ordered mass production of these to bring their people good fortune and gain favor for themselves. Japan's Empress Koken (718–70) had a million charms printed to ward off smallpox—but died as the project was completed, probably of smallpox! In C.E. 983 the Chinese printed the Buddhist **scriptures** in 5,048 separate volumes, totaling 130,000 pages, each page printed from a separately carved block.

A problem of language

In the 11th century, Korean and Chinese printers experimented with printing from single pieces of type put together in different combinations. In theory, their success was a big step forward because block printing could only produce the same whole page over and over again.

The *Diamond Sutra*, a Buddhist scripture, is one of the oldest complete printed books, with its known date of C.E. 868.

This 19th-century print shows people in China trimming and soaking bamboo to make paper.

In practice, however, this did not help much, because the Chinese, Japanese, and Korean alphabets are not made up of just a few letters, but rather of thousands of characters, each standing for a thing or an idea. To choose and put together a page from a huge store of characters, and then sort them out and put them back again, took a long time. In fact, it took so long that block printing was not much slower—especially when it was used for printing the same religious books over and over again, rather than producing new ones. In the end, therefore, this breakthrough came to nothing.

Paper

Paper was being used in China by C.E. 105. It was originally made from the inner bark of mulberry trees, which was soaked in water to make a pulp. This was pressed into sheets and dried. Later, old rags, rope, and even fishing nets were used. Coarser papers, made from straw or wood, were also manufactured, not for writing but for lanterns, fans, or wrapping. Chinese prisoners captured in Central Asia had brought the secret of paper making to the Arab world by C.E. 795. It reached Spain by the 12th century and then Italy and England by the 14th century. Paper was less beautiful than **parchment**, which was made of animal skin. It did not last nearly as long, but it was much, much cheaper.

Scribes and Scriptures

A little learning

Roman rule ended in Western Europe in the 5th century C.E. Towns and trade shrank. Almost the only literate people left were Christian priests, trained in **monasteries**. Each large monastery had a **scriptorium** where books were copied out by hand and novices (beginners) were taught to read and write. They still used Latin, the language of the Romans, for writing and worship.

Scribes usually wrote with goose-feather **quills** and ink made from soot and oil. They could copy up to four pages a day. They wrote on parchment made from the scraped skins of calves, sheep, or goats. A book of 350 pages would take the skins of 200 calves. Most monastery libraries had only a few dozen books, which they loaned to other libraries so they could all make their own copies.

Kings and nobles relied on scribes to keep records and accounts for them, to write letters, and to draw up **charters** and **treaties**. Latin was also used for all these purposes throughout Europe, no matter what language was spoken locally.

Eadwine, a Canterbury monk, drew this picture of himself working on a book of Psalms in about 1150.

English achievements

In England, King Alfred (849–899) had hand-copied books translated from Latin into English. This allowed more people to read them. He also ordered a **chronicle** of important events to be kept in English. England also produced one of the greatest books of the Middle Ages. In 1086 William I (about 1027–87) ordered a complete survey of the kingdom.

It was compiled by monks who usually spoke French, asked questions in English, and wrote in Latin. The people called the completed survey the *Domesday Book* (meaning "doomsday") because it reminded them of God calling everyone to account on the Day of Judgment.

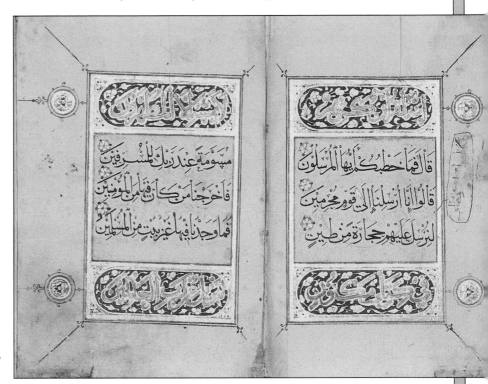

This Qur'an was handwritten in Turkey in the 14th century.

Sacred words

Throughout the Middle Ages, Christians and Muslims were often at war, but both religions agreed the most important books were those recording the words of God: the Bible and the Qur'an. Bibles and Qur'ans were written in beautiful **calligraphy** and bound in elaborate covers that were often decorated with gold or jewels.

In 698 Eadfrith, bishop of Lindisfarne, an island off the English coast, began copying out the four Gospels in Latin. It took him three years. Around C.E. 950 Aeldred, a monk, wrote an Anglo-Saxon translation between the lines of Eadfrith's text—the first Christian scripture in English.

Master Caxton's Hobby

A second career

William Caxton (about 1422–91) was an English merchant who lived in Bruges in Flanders (now part of Belgium) and in Westminster, near London. In his spare time, Caxton translated stories from French into English. He became interested in having them printed so that more of his friends could read them.

In 1472 Caxton brought a Gutenberg-style press from Cologne, Germany, to Bruges and began printing. His first book, translated into English by himself, was about the history of ancient Troy. He also printed one about chess. Retiring from business in 1476, Caxton brought a press back to England, setting it up in Westminster. Over the next fifteen years, he printed about 100 different books, including the poems of Geoffrey Chaucer and the stories of King Arthur and the Knights of the Round Table.

This illustrated page is from Chaucer's *Canterbury Tales*, printed by Caxton in 1483.

IMPRESSIO LIBRORVM.

Poteſt vt vna vox capi aure plurima :   *Linunt ita vna ſcripta mille paginas.*

Which English?

Caxton had to decide what sort of English to print. There was no standard form of the language. The words people used and the way they said them differed widely from region to region. Caxton himself wrote how a storm once forced two London merchants to stop in Kent only a few dozen miles downriver. When one asked a local farmer's wife to sell them eggs to eat, she said that she did not understand him because she could not speak French. He was angry because he did not speak French either! In Kent eggs were called *eyren*, which sounds very similar to their modern German name.

Caxton also noted, "Certaynly our langage now used varyeth ferre from that which was used and spoken when I was borne." When he was printing his books, Caxton used the English of London and southeast England. Over time, printing gradually fixed the spelling of words and made that particular dialect the basis of "standard English," as used by educated people and in public occasions.

Where to do business?

Caxton established his press and bookshop near London's Westminster Abbey because he thought its monks and visitors would be good customers. When he died he left his business to his assistant, Wynkyn de Worde (died 1535), who moved it to Fleet Street, in the central part of the city. He thought the rich merchants and nobles living there would be even better customers. For the next five centuries, Fleet Street and the area around St. Paul's Cathedral was the home of English printing and publishing.

Bibles and Beliefs

Luther

Throughout the Middle Ages, Christians in Western Europe obeyed the Roman Catholic Church, headed by the pope. Its teachings were based on the Bible but included many extra rules made by popes and councils of priests. Protestantism was a protest movement led by a German priest, Martin Luther (1483–1546). He said the Catholic Church was more concerned with wealth than saving souls. Luther argued that the Bible alone supplied correct Christian beliefs. This became the core Protestant idea. Luther translated the Bible from Latin into German so that more people could read it for themselves.

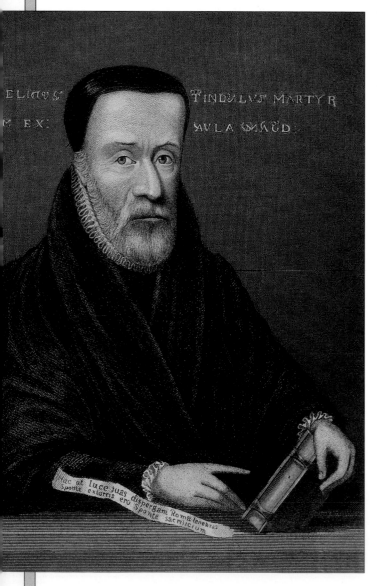

Reformation

A century earlier, the Bohemian Jan Hus (1370–1415) and Englishman John Wycliffe (about 1330–84) had held similar ideas to Luther, but they failed to start mass movements. Printing made all the difference. The cheap Bibles first printed in Germany—as a result of Gutenberg's work—spread Protestantism into neighboring Switzerland, France, Holland, and Great Britain. This became known as the Reformation because Protestants set up separate, reformed churches. They refused to obey the pope and followed new ways of worshipping, based on the Bible. Protestant worship stressed study of the Bible, with preachers explaining its meaning in **sermons**.

William Tyndale (1494–1536) translated the New Testament into English. He knew Luther and Gutenberg's assistant, Schoffer. In 1536 Tyndale was burned at the stake for **heresy**.

Books and belief

Most people were too poor to own books, but if a Protestant family did have one, it was a Bible. It was certainly the book everybody, literate or not, knew best. It affected the language people used, from everyday speech to poetry. Luther's Bible set the standard for how German should be written.

For two centuries after Luther, Europe was divided by religious wars between Catholics and Protestants and between different kinds of Protestants. One of the main reasons people began to emigrate to the United States was so that they would be free to worship in their own way.

This picture from a 19th-century edition of Foxe's *Book of Martyrs* shows two Protestant bishops, Latimer and Ridley, being burned in 1555, during the reign of Britain's Catholic Queen Mary I.

Best-sellers

Religion was the main subject of the most famous books printed during this period. After the Bible, the most popular book in England at the time was Foxe's *Book of Martyrs* (first published in 1554), about Protestants who had died for their beliefs. John Milton's long poem *Paradise Lost* explains how Satan, originally an angel, was thrown out of heaven. John Bunyan's *The Pilgrim's Progress* tells how its hero, Christian, comes through many dangers and evils to reach heaven at last.

Printing the World

Secret knowledge

Printing made books cheaper and more plentiful, but this did not mean the information in them was more accurate. This was even more true of maps. Before printing was developed, maps were drawn by hand. This made it easier to control how many were produced and circulated. As trading countries, such as Portugal and the Netherlands, grew rich bringing spices from Asia, they tried to keep knowledge about the sea routes to Asia to themselves. After Englishman Francis Drake sailed around the world (1577–80), his **logbook** was kept top secret and no mention of his adventure appeared in print for over ten years. Long after printing developed, seamen continued to rely on hand-drawn maps as being more reliable, easier to keep updated—and secret.

Profit before truth

Early printed maps were produced using engraved blocks of wood. After about 1550, the wooden blocks were replaced by copper printing plates. These were very expensive to prepare. Printers often refused to throw them away, even after new geographical discoveries. Sometimes they just kept printing the same old maps. Sometimes they even sold them alongside newer ones that contradicted them. A Portuguese ship sailed around Africa into the Indian Ocean in 1497, but maps ignoring this sea route to India were still being sold in 1570.

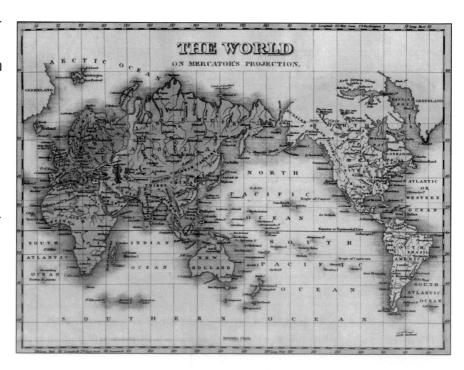

This 19th-century map shows how the Flemish mapmaker Geradus Mercator (1512–94) changed our way of looking at the world, by treating it as a stretched-out globe.

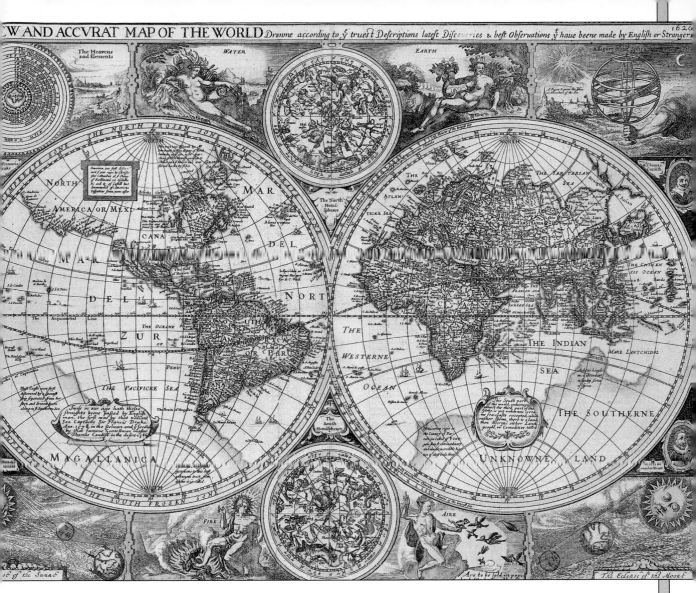

An English world map, first drawn around 1610, pays tribute to Drake and other explorers.

Naming America

Italian-born Amerigo Vespucci (1451–1512) sold supplies to Christopher Columbus before himself voyaging to explore the coast of South America. He wrote a private letter in Italian describing his travels, which was later printed in Latin.

In 1507 Martin Waldseemüller (1470–1518), a German amateur printer, published a description of the world, including a large map printed from twelve wooden blocks, which drew on the Latin version of Amerigo Vespucci's letter. It was Waldseemüller who decided that the newly discovered continent described by Vespucci should be called "America" in his honor. Later he decided that Vespucci did not deserve the credit. He left out the name America on his next three maps, but it was too late. He had already sold 1,000 copies of the first version, so the name stuck.

15

Read All About It!

Before newspapers were produced, merchants and bankers who needed to know what was going on in the world paid for regular "intelligencers" or "courants"—handwritten reports of the latest news from important cities.

Germany leads

The world's first newspaper, *Relation*, was published in Strasbourg (now in France) in 1609, although the German *Avisa Relation* was a close second. The German *Leipziger Journal*, launched as a weekly in 1660, soon became the world's first daily newspaper. The *Wiener Zeitung*, first published in Vienna, Austria, in 1703, is the oldest newspaper still being printed.

England catches up

In the 1620s, Dutch printers began to send over to England "corantos," which were cheaply printed pamphlets of foreign news. During Britain's civil wars (1642–49), government control of printing broke down. Thousands of pamphlets were printed, all putting forward different political and religious points of view. By the late 1600s, printed news-sheets were being circulated regularly in London coffeehouses, where men met for business. Their most important news was about ships' cargoes. London's first regular daily newspaper was the *Daily Courant*, published between 1702 and 1735. Newspapers soon appeared in **provincial** cities, including Norwich, Bristol, Worcester, and Exeter. By 1760 there were four London dailies; by 1790 there were fourteen. The number of provincial papers, usually published weekly, rose from 35 in 1760 to 150 by 1821.

The London Malignants difarmed, (89)
Fifty thoufand pounds to be raifed,
The Lord Capels Forces difperfed,
The Cavaliers from Glocefter repulfed.

Numb. 12

Mercurius Civicus.
LONDONS
INTELLIGENCER:
OR,
Truth impartially related from thence to the whole Kingdome, to prevent mif-information.

From *Friday Auguft 11. to Thurfday Auguft 17. 1643.*

Oth Houfes of Parliament and the City of London, have a long time been much indangered through the Plots and confpiracies of many malignant Inhabitants in that City, the Suburbs, and parts adjacent; notwithftanding which, that City, which in many other things of great confequence to this Nation both in former and latter time, hath af-

M   forded

A 1643 issue of a weekly paper published in London carries news of the civil war.

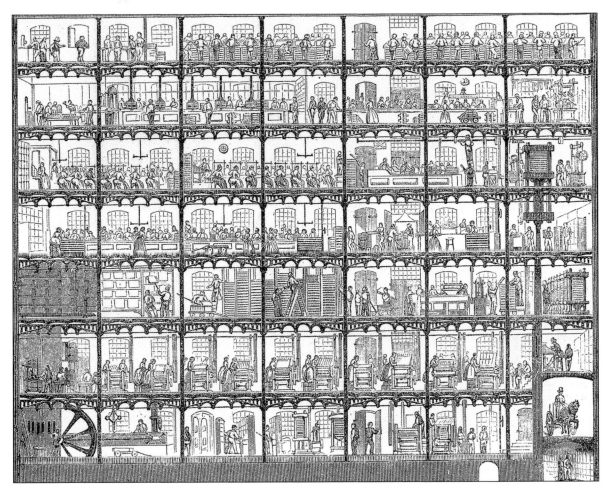

This illustration from *Harper's New Monthly Magazine* shows how it was produced in New York in 1865. Notice the many women working there.

The United States

The American colonies' earliest newspaper, *Publick Occurrences*, appeared in 1690 and was banned by the government after one issue! In 1704 Scottish printer John Campbell began publishing a weekly *Boston Newsletter*. He took two-thirds of its contents from London papers, filling the rest with shipping news, law-court proceedings, parts of sermons, and brief notices about storms, deaths, and other dramatic events.

Power of the press

By the 19th century, governments were increasingly chosen by voters rather than rulers. Newspaper reports of speeches and debates became an important link between politicians and voters. Newspapers' **editorial** columns and letters pages gave politicians feedback on public opinion about events and policies. Many political parties linked themselves with particular newspapers. Newspapers also investigated **scandals** and injustices, which the public then expected governments to address.

Prominent Printers

Before the 20th century, printing was the main form of communication. Many printers were very successful and became rich and powerful.

Inventor

Boston-born Benjamin Franklin (1706–90) invented the lightning conductor, bifocal lenses, and a stove. He also helped to write the Declaration of Independence and Constitution. Before all of those achievements, Franklin was a printer. From 1724 to 1726, Franklin worked in London, the greatest center for printing in the English-speaking world. Returning to America, he won the contract to print paper money for Pennsylvania. He later printed official documents for New Jersey, Maryland, and Delaware as well.

In 1729 he started a newspaper, the *Pennsylvania Gazette*. Between 1732 and 1758, each year he published an edition of *Poor Richard's Almanack*, a practical encyclopaedia containing **astronomical** information and farming notes, mixed in with verses and jokes. Franklin also set up Philadelphia's first library and an academy that became the University of Pennsylvania.

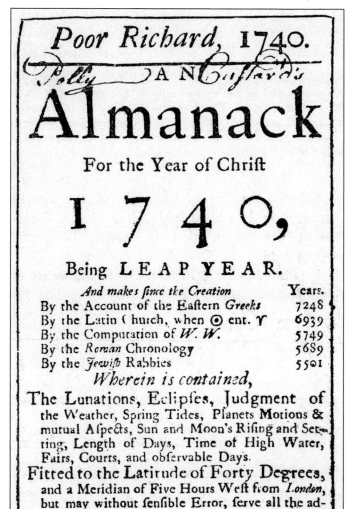

Benjamin Franklin's *Poor Richard's Almanack* became the only other book besides the Bible in many colonial American homes.

Writer

Samuel Richardson (1689–1761) had a
business just off Fleet Street, the center
of London's printing trade. He produced
books, magazines, advertising posters,
letterheads, and business cards. In
1723 he took over printing a political
newspaper, the *True Briton*, and in
1733 began printing for the House of
Commons, a part of the British
Parliament. In 1739–40 he wrote and
published a novel, *Pamela*, that was
widely praised. In France it was made into
a play. Another novel, *Clarissa*, was
translated into French, Dutch, and
German. In 1754–55 Richardson served
as master of the Stationers' Company—in effect, the
head of the printing profession in Britain.

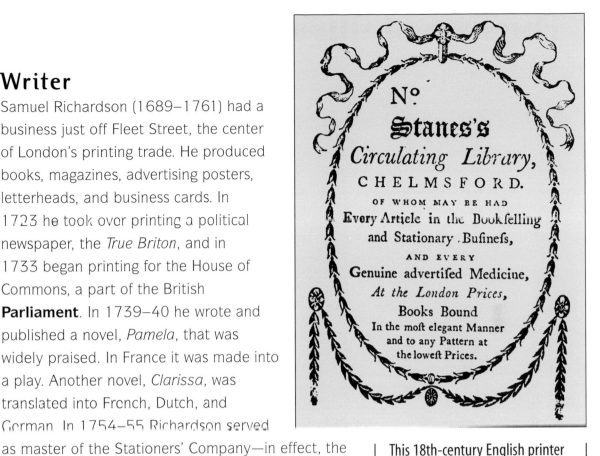

This 18th-century English printer
sold stationery and medicines, in
addition to typesetting, binding,
and loaning books.

Family businesses

Luke Hansard (1752–1828) took on responsibility
for printing for the House of Commons when he was
only 22, and this became the family business. His
son Thomas (1776–1833) wrote a history and
handbook of printing. The reports of House of
Commons debates became known simply as
Hansard and are still called this today.

Thomas De La Rue (1793–1866) began by making
ladies' summer bonnets out of paper and went on to
print headed stationery, playing cards, checks, and
stamps. Warren De La Rue (1815–89) invented an
envelope-making machine and in his leisure time
pioneered astronomical photography. Sir Thomas
De La Rue (1849–1911) made the firm a worldwide
business, printing stamps and paper money for many
different countries.

The Rise of the Writer

Benjamin Franklin and Samuel Richardson were businessmen first and writers second. As more people learned to read and write and had spare time to read for pleasure, it became possible to make a full-time living just from writing.

Fame...

Englishman Samuel Johnson (1709–84) compiled the first true dictionary of the English language (1755), which made him famous. In the U.S., the *American Spelling Book* was published in 1783 by Noah Webster (1758–1843), who created the first dictionary of American English. The book sold about 100 million copies over the following century.

A generation later in Britain, poets Percy Bysshe Shelley (1792–1822), John Keats (1795–1821), and Lord Byron (1788–1824) all found lasting fame. Novelist Jane Austen (1775–1817) was praised by Sir Walter Scott.

Alice in Wonderland **was originally written in a diary, with pictures by the author, Lewis Carroll.**

Scott (1771–1832) was the best-selling British writer of his day. In the U.S., James Fenimore Cooper (1789–1851) gained fame for his tales of frontiersmen. William Holmes McGuffey's (1800–73) "readers," compiled from 1853 onward to teach reading to Americans, sold over 125 million copies.

...and fortune

Writing novels raised British authors Charles Dickens (1812–70) and W. M. Thackeray (1811–63) to fame and fortune. Anthony Trollope (1815–82) worked as a post office official and, writing each morning before he went to work, produced 47 books to raise extra money to support his family. Washington Irving (1783–1859), creator of "Rip Van Winkle," was the first U.S. writer to become famous outside the United States. Mark Twain (1835–1910)—printer, riverboat pilot, gold-miner, editor— drew on his adventures in humorous novels that made him popular in the United States and abroad. Best-selling authors since 1900 include U.S. child-care expert Dr. Benjamin Spock, the English novelist George Orwell, the U.S. author John Grisham, and the U.S. author Toni Morrison.

U.S. author Mark Twain on the day he received an honorary degree from Oxford University, in England.

For younger readers

Some of the world's best-selling books have been written mainly for younger readers. They include Lewis Carroll's *Alice in Wonderland* (1865) and Beatrix Potter's *The Tale of Peter Rabbit* (1902). Other best-selling modern children's authors include Dr. Seuss (Theodor Geisel), the creator of *The Cat in the Hat*; E. B. White, the creator of *Charlotte's Web*; Louise Fitzhugh, the author of *Harriet the Spy*; Maurice Sendak, the creator of *Where the Wild Things Are*; Judy Blume, the creator of *Are You There God? It's Me, Margaret*; and J. K. Rowling, creator of the "Harry Potter" series.

Prints, Posters, Packaging

Profitable prints

English artist William Hogarth (1697–1764) trained as an **engraver**. Hogarth became successful by painting scenes of London life and then turning them into engravings. Instead of selling one expensive picture to one buyer, he could sell hundreds of cheap printed copies to many buyers. In 1735 he persuaded the British Parliament to pass a law giving artists **copyright** to their pictures, just like authors had with their books.

Publishers found a good market for books of prints showing beautiful natural views, the homes of the wealthy, and scenes of foreign travel. Around 1800 the English cartoonists James Gillray, Thomas Rowlandson, and George Cruikshank produced hundreds of **caricatures** attacking the politicians and fashionable leaders of society. In the U.S., by the mid-1800s David Claypoole Johnston and Thomas Nast also became known for their caricatures.

CASTLE ACRE MONASTERY, *in* NORFOLK.

Prints of ruins were in demand, since picturesque views were very fashionable and popular.

Print for profits

As populations, incomes, and literacy all expanded rapidly in the 19th century, huge printing opportunities opened up to supply the needs of businesses for bills, receipts, **ledgers**, and labels. The increased use of paper money produced a need for banknotes that were difficult to **forge**. Railroad, steamship, and bus companies needed tickets. More and more foodstuffs and medicines were sold in sealed packages, which carried printed information or advertising. In 1840 Britain issued the world's first pre-paid sticky postage stamps. Other countries quickly copied the idea. From the 1880s onward, there was a need for telephone directories. Specialized businesses emerged producing, for example, tickets numbered in sequence or invitation cards printed in gold.

Posters, politics, and pleasure

The first posters were government announcements of new laws, taxes, or chances to join the army. As more people could read and vote, political parties began to use posters to get support. Theaters used posters to attract audiences. In France, clubs, restaurants, exhibitions, and galleries employed artists to design pictorial posters. Posters by artists such as Jules Chéret (1836–1932), Henri Toulouse-Lautrec (1864–1901), or Alphonse Mucha (1860–1939) are now regarded as important works of art. In the U.S., Will Bradley (1868–1962) became known for his posters.

Cheap posters using many different typefaces brought regular income to provincial printers.

Better and Better, Faster and Faster

Faster, clearer, brighter

Gutenberg could print 300 sheets a day. By 1620 **counterweighted** presses had raised this to 150 an hour. Steam presses appeared in the 19th century, and then high-speed rotary presses turned out 8,000 sheets an hour. Finally, in the 20th-century, the offset printer that turns out today's newspapers at the rate of 70,000 sheets an hour was invented in the U.S. (see page 25). Different typefaces made print easier and more interesting to read, and from the 18th century it became possible to print in color.

Spreading the word

Printing spread very rapidly, so that by 1500 there were millions of books in circulation. Sixteenth-century Germany alone produced 45,000 new titles. This revolution in communication had an enormous impact. It spread new ideas—especially about religion and politics—across Europe and helped change people's thinking forever.

The Stanhope press, invented in 1800, could print much bigger sheets than earlier presses much more quickly.

Typesetters work in a newspaper office around 1900. The work was skilled, clean, and well paid.

Invention by accident

In 1904 the New York printer Ira Rubel noticed that when a rubber pad was pressed against an inky metal printing plate, the image was transferred clearly to the pad. Moreover, the image printed from the pad was clearer than that printed from the plate. In this way, "offset" printing was born. Using rotating, rubber-coated cylinders, the printing process was sped up considerably.

Invention by design

The next major printing breakthrough was in the way **compositors** set lines of type ready for printing. By the 20th century, they did this on machines like large computer keyboards. Then, in 1939, the American William Heubner invented a photographic way of setting the characters to make up words. Phototypesetting made the job much quicker, allowing 1,000 characters to be set per minute.

The electronic revolution

In 1947 a U.S. firm made a electronic scanner that engraved an image directly onto the printing surface. Computer-controlled printing began to emerge in the 1960s. Even so, during the 1970s printing was still quite a slow process, using bulky and expensive reels of film.

Microchip technology changed all that. By the 1990s, nearly all books were written and designed on computer and sent electronically directly to the printer. Sophisticated software, such as PageMaker (1985), made design easier, and cheap printers allowed people to produce high-quality printing at home. Today, many documents—including books—are never printed at all, but rather published directly on disk or onto the Internet.

Back to Beautiful Books

The use of steam-powered machinery to print books on paper made from wood pulp, and to bind them in cotton or cardboard covers, meant that more people could afford them. The books themselves, however, were not pretty to look at or handle. Cheap ink faded. Cheap paper cracked. Cheap bindings and covers were easily torn or fell apart.

Crusade for beauty

When he was in his fifties, English artist and poet William Morris (1834–96) decided to revive the art of making fine books. He was already rich enough to finance his hobby and was also qualified for the task. Morris was famous for designing wallpapers and textiles. He was also a superb calligrapher, an expert on English literature, and the owner of a fine collection of old books and manuscripts. Morris had strong views about art and work. He believed beautiful things would only be produced by craftsmen who enjoyed their work and took pride in it.

This Kelmscott Chaucer is on display at William Morris's childhood home, Water House, in East London.

Morris founded the Kelmscott Press in 1891 in his house in London and printed 52 different titles. His greatest achievement was an edition of Geoffrey Chaucer's *Canterbury Tales*. Morris himself designed the typeface, based on 15th-century writing styles. His friend, the artist Edward Burne-Jones, did the illustrations. Each page was meant to be as pleasing as a picture.

Private presses

The Kelmscott Press inspired the founding of other private printing presses. Their aim was not to make money but to present the best of literature in the best possible way. C. R. Ashbee, a follower of Morris, took over his printing press to found Essex House Press (1898–1910) in London's East End. Charles Ricketts's Vale Press (1896–1903) printed all of Shakespeare's works in 39 volumes. French artist Lucien Pissarro took over the Vale Press types for his Eragny Press, which introduced elegant patterned paper bindings. The Doves Press (1901–20) produced a splendid five-volume Bible for use in churches.

20th-century printers and typographers

Bruce Rogers (1870–1957), one of the United States' greatest book designers, created the Centaur typeface used by the Metropolitan Museum of Art, and he also worked with Harvard University Press. Other important U.S. printers and typographers in the early 20th century included Frederic W. Goudy (1865–1947) and Morris F. Benton (1872–1948). In San Francisco, Edwin and Robert Grabhorn printed books for the Book Club of California. English engraver Eric Gill (1882–1940) is probably best remembered as the designer of the typeface known as Gill Sans Serif.

This is a sentence written in

CENTAUR TYPE FACE

designed by Bruce Rogers in 1915.

The Great Debate

Exaggerated effect?

Many historians claim that printing was the *cause* of widespread change in Europe. However, some say that is was more of a *sign* of change. There is also discussion about whether printing is now outdated technology. Below are arguments for both sides.

Question 1: Did the spread of printing bring about fundamental changes in European society, religion, and politics?

Yes!

- Printing enabled Luther's Reformation to spread and succeed where Hus and Wycliffe had failed (see page 12).

- It encouraged and enabled the spread of literacy and education.

- It allowed the ideas of the 17th-century Scientific Revolution to be distributed widely, quickly, and cheaply.

- It enabled political groups to publish their ideas, leading to the formation of political parties in the late 17th century.

No!

- Many of the major changes of the early modern period—the Renaissance and Europe's discovery of America, for instance—had nothing to do with printing.

- Printing was developed to meet the need for more books as a result of improved education and greater literacy. In other words, printing was more a result of change than a cause of it.

- As Christianity and Islam had spread without printing, there is no reason why Protestantism should not have done the same.

What do you think?

| Books being sold during the Reformation. How far did printing lead to change? |

The death of the book

Question 2: Is it likely that electronic publishing (on disc, on TV, and on the Internet) will mean the end of the printed book in a few years?

Yes!

- Technology will soon produce devices that are just as handy and reliable as books.
- Books are environmentally unfriendly, since they require trees to be cut down to make the paper.
- Reference books have already been largely replaced by CDs and the Internet.
- Electronic means of delivery make text more interactive and fun.

No!

- Books are still far more practical than any of the alternatives, and are likely to remain so for years to come.
- They are infinitely flexible, requiring no batteries or electricity—nothing in fact but a pair of eyes.
- Books are much more personal than electronic devices. They look and feel good and are fun to collect.
- They are cheap, tough, and long-lasting.

What do you think?

Computers are used in the classroom. Will they eventually replace books completely?

Find Out More

Using the Internet
Explore the Internet to find out more about the printing press. You can use a search engine, such as www.yahooligans.com or www.google.com, and type in keywords such as *Benjamin Franklin*, *printing press*, or *Gutenberg*.

More Books to Read
Chambers, Catherine. *Behind Media: Newspapers*. Chicago: Heinemann Library, 2001.

Heinrichs, Ann. *Benjamin Franklin: Printer, Scientist, Author*.
    Chanhassen, Minn.: Child's World, 2004.

Parker, Steve. *20th-Century Media*. Milwaukee: Gareth Stevens, 2002.

Timeline

105	Paper known to be in use in China
698–700	*Lindisfarne Gospel* copied by Bishop Eadfrith
795	Paper making known in Baghdad, Iraq
983	Chinese print the complete Buddhist scriptures
1086	*Domesday Book* compiled in England
1455	*Gutenberg Bible* printed
1468	Death of Johannes Gutenberg
1476	William Caxton brings printing to England
1501	Italic typeface introduced
1507	Waldseemüller names America
1522	Luther translates New Testament from Greek and Hebrew into German
1525	William Tyndale's English translation of the New Testament is printed in Cologne
1534	Luther translates entire Bible into German
1554	Foxe's *Book of Martyrs* published
1588	Bible printed in Welsh
1609	World's first newspaper published in Strasbourg
1615	*Frankfurter Journal* published
1620	Blaeu's counterweighted press introduced
1642	Mezzotint process invented
1702	*Daily Courant*, London's first regular daily newspaper, published
1703	*Wiener Zeitung* published in Vienna; it is still being printed
1704	*Boston Newsletter* published in American colonies
1719	Full-color printing pioneered in Germany
1732	Benjamin Franklin begins publishing *Poor Richard's Almanack*
1735	Hogarth persuades British Parliament to pass Copyright Act
1755	Samuel Johnson's *Dictionary* completed
1774	Luke Hansard prints the debates of the British House of Commons
1783	Noah Webster publishes *American Spelling Book*
1799	Machine for making paper as a roll, not sheets, invented in France
1816	Koenig steam-powered rotary press perfected
1840	Penny Black postage stamp issued in Britain
1848	Rotary presses produce 8,000 copies per hour
1891	William Morris founds the Kelmscott Press
1904	Ira Rubel pioneers offset printing
1939	William Heubner pioneers phototypesetting
1982	Electronic page-making introduced
1990	First handheld computers produced
2000	Stephen King publishes short story straight onto Internet

Glossary

alloy	mixture of metals
antimony	poisonous, silvery white metal used in casting type
astronomical	relating to the science of the movements of stars and planets
calligraphy	art of beautiful writing
caricature	cartoon exaggerating faces and features
cast	make an object by pouring hot metal into a mold
charter	legal document granting right to hold land or do business
chronicle	official record of important events
compositor	person who composes type into pages ready for printing
copyright	legal ownership of the right to reproduce a book or work of art
counterweight	weight suspended near the end of a moving part of a machine that makes it easier to work the machine
editorial	parts of a newspaper written by the people who run it, giving their opinions on the news
engraver	someone who carves designs into printing plates
forge	to make an illegal copy of something valuable, such as money
heresy	having beliefs that do not agree with those of the church
ledger	large book for keeping accounts of money earned and paid out
literate	able to read and write
logbook	official record of a voyage kept by the captain of a ship
monastery	community of monks
parchment	fine writing surface made by scraping and cleaning animal skin
parliament	group responsible for making laws in some countries
provincial	relating to the areas other than the capital city of a country
quill	pen made from a bird's feather that is cut to a point
scandal	event most people would believe to be immoral
scribe	person who makes a living by copying documents or writing letters for others
scriptorium	writing room of a monastery, usually located where it can catch bright light from the north
scriptures	sacred writings of a religion
sermon	talk given by a church leader and based on the Bible, to explain how Christians should behave
treaty	formal agreement, often between two countries
type	small block of metal cast in relief to bear a letter or mark used in printing
typeface	set of type made to a particular style or size
typographer	person who makes typefaces

Index